WITHIN REACH

Russell Erwin

WITHIN REACH

I. "AND WHERE ARE YOU?"

Villawood Primary, 1959

i. When playgrounds were gravel

Unceasing—the industrial work of cicadas.
Jet engines held at pitch, jaws chewing
through warehouses of heat. We are saturated.
Our heads, thick with eucalyptus.
Suddenly, air, dense in silence,
as is a gorge, midday.
Then, as suddenly, eruption. It resumes.
Our heads whirring. Giddy-silly.

I am face-down in the gravel
as about, boys whirl in a flock.
One changes direction. They swoop
to the other end of that yard's empire
in a whooping fantasy, as overhead,
cockatoos tear the air into strips,
hanging bark-like, as they abscond,
careless as vandals.

Along wooden seats beneath the eaves
girls hive, some playing bones, some skip,
stepping in and out to the looping discipline of a rhyme,
some close around a serious whisper
like petals of the one flower.
Some watch, learning.

Sixty-ish now, I have not forgotten that taste:
—stones in my mouth.
There is blood, its salt, caking my hair.

And in the empty acres
of the yard, something clear.
By the wall the girls exchange places,
giggle, squabble, in a kind of dance.
One though, at the edge, looks across
the yard, the years, at me.
Her eyes stay a moment long.
She knew the cost of play.

ii. For some reason in a corridor, after school

Into those wooden floors was buffed
a pleasant citrus smell. At an angle
light in a sheet, mirror-cold, like "Flood on the Darling".
High up were fixed windows, offering samples of sky,
hinting at something beyond.
And lingering, those clotted smells: wet wool,
the foreignness of other children's bodies,
the houses from where they'd come, hair oil,
leather satchels. Or lovelier, by her desk,
Miss Rosemary's perfume.

And one afternoon the school deserted
—only the cleaner hosing out bins
blackened in their mould—smell of oranges,
the incinerator sour and smouldering,
a couple of dogs biting at a willy-willy,
nosing for scraps, then tearing off.
Inside, the empty rooms neat as a model.
Everywhere, light: clinical, uncomplicated.
Each chair and desk, single and distinct.
And silent. Any sound, answering itself,
while from out there, somewhere,
peewits, their small pinching cries,
sudden, then gone. Farther off,
the murmur of traffic on a highway, beyond knowing.

As if entering slyly by a side door,
words insinuated—those in black
on the *Daily Mirror*'s posters,
or in the anxious code my parents used.
Speaking, as did that blanket,
in the Police Exhibit at the Easter Show
so close, and mute
"Graham Thorne", "Kidnapped".

In that empty corridor, a name spoke.
This was no place to be.

iii. An introduction to art: among others, Murillo

Along the walls just above child height prints—
Drysdale—his hard-bitter-sour colour,
his withered figures; Dobell's Wangi,
the palette scowling blue-black and cold
as the psalmist Heysen, our Samuel Palmer,
—hosannas golden through temple columns of red gums.
A Namatjira, eaten by the afternoon sun.
Even so, innocence in the lightning-white
of those ghost gums. Others—
Van Gogh's whorled stars, furnace-white,
Utrillo's gaunt, leafless Notre Dame,
its snow, an oddity on Villawood's summer walls.

Most sensual, most disturbing though
—melons, peelings and rind, grapes dangled
above a mouth, and death-grubby urchins,
grained in their poverty. A knife, rags of clothes,
flesh, eyes, hunger.

A lifetime on, thinking of those boys
—juice dribbling rare delight.
I sense eyes, and a hunger not theirs.

iv. Classmates

In the playground, among the simple names, kids from Villawood Hostel, their funny first names, funny voices, or no voice at all—Poms, the Poles, the Yugoslavs, Dagoes, Wops. Yuri, in callipers, the cage polio forced him into, so that he crossed the playground rocking like a toy, so slowly it made him seem wise. The Egyptian boy, Nasi, who derailed a train, fierce as a rat, eyes swivelling, always alert for something, as if he were aware of alleyways and shadows, a memory of hunger, a smile's snare; the red-haired Welsh boy, Gareth, lanky and flopping like the bean tendrils of his consonants, the soft doona of his vowels—could something this gentle ever persist? Wild boy Charles of the bottle-glasses and the man's voice, whom everybody avoided because he was mad, who exposed himself and laughed, and laughed as he sprayed like a bull; and Luba, 'from Cuba' we chanted, shy as a native of the Amazon, broad-boned and in pain because she couldn't hide, trying to blend where there was no foliage, remembered only because of her name and that she was just right for a kind of cruelty; and the girl who has now lost her name—Jean?—Joan?—whom the teacher picked on because she'd had lice, didn't have a uniform, hadn't gone to Mass, was small, a downy darkness shading her upper lip, who scurried, seemed grimy, was Italian. She, who was hunted, so he could win over a class of eleven-year-olds. We despised her for making us into such easy cowards.

Villier's Road, Moss Vale

The half mile to the corner,
the wind, the cold ocean of it,
stripping the left side of your face.
Turn right, the long stretch down the hill,
the wind baying. The power lines.
sway, sway.
                    "It's time for you to go",
she said, that coiffed woman, his mother,
disappointed we'd become friends.
Their house, snug beneath pines.
Dark, seasoned floors, French windows.
A baby grand, stables, pony gear.

A yellow light
                    and then, not.
That first slap of cold.

Out of the dark, darker forms plunge
at the wire, trample, tear the earth.
So near. Smell the steam of their heat.
Pressed, the fence gives.
Flicked, a barb pings.

And where are you?

Near the Buddhist Monastery, Bundanoon

Morning: the bush is cold.
Leaves overhanging the road
are leather-stiff, dull
as if dressed with fat.
A caprice of wind
and in a spray,
a shattering of glitter.
Thornbills and wrens burst
from a thicket of tea-tree.

Passing, I see a termite mound,
earth-brown, sandstone-worn.
It moves! A man there
walking toward town,
a book under his arm.
Surprised, I wave.
He does not.

Like the bush
in the discipline
of its one dress,
he is sufficient to be,
clothed
in whatever
this day is.

Knowing Grace Kelly

for Kerry Armstrong

You were my Grace Kelly,
tho' only vaguely knowing who she was.
Surely you guessed
it wasn't coincidence
a textbook would fall
as you'd walk by a library desk.

In those mini-skirt days,
your panty-hose legs lengthened
to something very like heaven …
And your pale blonde hair,

purely Nordic. Your poise—
terrifying and remote,
which now you say was shyness.

At the class reunion after thirty years
you said what I never expected,
"I came because I wanted to see you again."
Wow! Heartfelt thanks for that.

There's the distance of years
—still, you knock me back to gawkiness
with your calm, the steady assessment
of your attention, your care.

And like that schoolboy, my heart skips
along streets newly found,
repeating your words like a promise,
blossoming and giddy, hoping

here might be the beginnings
of a friendship with Grace Kelly.

Party Line, Yeoval 16-K

for Brab

Three shorts and one long,
                                        or was that 16-D?
What was yours? They all could tell
who was ringing simply by the way
the handle had been rung.
                                "That's the Vaughans.
                                Must be in for the evening."

Then we'd notice there weren't any rings.
The line down—a tin insulator jammed into a tree
worked loose or a lightning strike, we'd walk
almost all the way to the Wellington-Parkes Road,
propping the bellied line, replacing breaks
with bits of No.8.
                                And once,
among the glitter of longnecks flung by shearers
after weeks out there, or what immortal boys,
wasted after a B&S, had sprayed, writing-off a new ute,
—a pink baby's jumpsuit, nestled in its tissue paper,
and on the card, just made out "Sorry, I … "
and guilty, left it, curled around its story.

This single wire threaded a district, rung it
with voices—the unalterable fact of prices,
gossip, a young wife's anxious chat,
fire out in the hills, "Will get you to
shift those ewes. No hurry."

It felt good coming home.
That night, the line we'd repaired tinkled
in its code. Ringing long, short, long.
That wire we'd held in our hands
would sing the birth of your daughters,
and one Sunday morning, a world wrung
empty—their mother, your wife, Wendy, dead.
The line ringing long: long, short, long.

"Lochlands", Yeoval (a paean)

Single man's quarters—lino and masonite kitchen,
horse gear on the verandah, marking pliers on the table,
The Pastoral Review stacked in a corner.
A skin of fibro away, a frost hardening, and the stars.
Each season with its perfume and air: musk-damp
thick in the hollow below the house;
the 'gonk-gonk' of frogs, viscous as a mud pool,
almost till dawn; wethers nosing along the fence,
shifting through the night.
                                        Spring: scented froth
in its heady over-the-top breakout from winter.
Or once again, paddocks haying-off in a bob-tail fizzle.
Bountiful summers—like an unexpected Christmas gift.
Waiting for the autumn break—accepting
what it meant when it didn't. At first, "'S a bit dry",
then as drought—wearing as a bedside vigil
—rhythmless—it the measure of your character.
Ironbark in blossom, the crucifying burr,
the flooded creek shining like new metal,
surprising in its crescent like a smile.

This country keeps to itself.

Cupped in a dazed blue, the near distance
grained in olive-grey like an old painting.
Earth-scent, wool-smell, death-stink.
Its languages, the observing eye, skill.
Deft. Just so.

Dogs, good or retired—none other.
Heads of cattle, lifting as you pass.
Over cauliflower curds of backs, the kelpie sinks
into plump cushions in a packed yard at shearing,
and bobs up, grinning.
Through the unshaven stubble
of black cypress hills, under twisted hammer beams
of yellow box, the road a creek. And, in between,
the king-hit slam. Magnesium-white. Nuclear sunlight.

A broken windmill, its shaft clanking,
blades whirring in any shift of air.
Squabbling—galahs flare from a dead box,
then return through their screams, settle,
gossiping in the grey down of dusk.
Of grubbing stumps, and on dark,
we returning, pass their towering in flame.
Cold stripping breath from our faces.

Company, First Night on the Main Range

Adam-naked, white as toothpaste,
the slink of him along the bonnet of a vee dub,
his shaved head surfacing like Foo from a book
—Dostoyevsky, of course—sun-dazed, hash-glazed.

This was as 'alternative'
as a timid boy could have imagined,
out there, beneath those unsullied skies,
first night in one of the mustering huts.

That night: the river in early spate burbled,
happy as an infant; the easy gabble of strangers
swapping whatever lies were needed
while I retreated beyond the firelight.

Hours settled into their embers until,
the way a cinema floods with light,
the door gaped. In the moonlight, a German,
his skin aglow, beaming like an ebullient god,

triumphant like Jaeger, like Nimrod,
towering heraldic, a trout glistening
in each hand, his eel-sleek girlfriend clinging,
indivisible from his shadow.

That night, long as a Russian winter,
sleep fell forfeit to the rise and fall
of schnapps-bold boast-talk, words
like bottles flung from a *droshky*.

Later, from a sleeping bag burrow,
the friction of skin on murmuring skin,
syllables of a river in its flow,
while in my head the fantastic flamed

like haze rippling over coals. I praying
that *Crime and Punishment* would keep
within its pages, or, that I was a fisherman,
wading thigh-deep in a whisky-clear water;

my hands, those her trout-sleek skin
would yield to, wriggling.

II. “BOTH OF YOU, THERE”

In the Hallway of My Parents' House

I get up and go down the hall,
past where from shadows
menace suggested itself,
where voices late at night
meant disruption: an accident,
a death, sometimes joy.

I stand where I'd hared in and out.
Moonlight pales at my feet.
Like a negative, the kitchen is ashen,
the lino flour-white. Dishes racked.
A bowl, a plate, a cup. His cutlery.
The pantry—dry bread stale. Past
the bathroom, scent weakly floral, clinging.

Tonight, I am under a roof
anodyne as any motel.
The hours work their way
through the house, obedient,
as ever, to his schedule.
Nothing unusual but
I'm the one up, awake.

My father, asleep
in their room which he keeps neat.
My father, at last, asleep
in the home they had made,
where he keeps house,
neat and waiting.

Bedside, April 6th

At your bed watching you,
as you watched over me.
You are beyond me now.
You rally, relapse.

Why struggle as if bound
against your will? Surely
a life of faith means His Hand
is near. The light you trusted,
welcoming, secure.

Your faith always
the greater part of you.
Whatever He is
lived through you.
You are what I am not:
untroubled by doubt, sure.

Seeing you resist
what I thought
you did not fear
I see you clear.
You—a son.
Your father nowhere near,
which nothing
can reassure.

Benediction

Inside his last hours
words trying to connect.
That sense might be restored:
he to his life, him to us.

His voice, hoarse, thrashing,
"You can't wait.
Can you,
till I'm gone."

Not one for words,
his benediction.

Volta

for my parents

I flip a rectangle of white card.
And there—the way the opening image
instantly fills a screen—are you two,
whom I cannot forget,
who every day I do.

Desperate, I rush to recall
what I can, hollowed,
that I've allowed this to slip.

Both of you, there,
alive in what I hold.
What I know
I cannot believe.
You are not here.

Your decency and shy love
breathes and says you were.
You were. I cannot look
for very long.

Approaching your age,
I hear the voices
of my grown children,
and the generation following them.
It doesn't alter the scale of loss.

Knitting

A nurse notices my jumper, examines the work,
—the tension, the evenness of its stitches,
how the sleeves had been set in. Asks
"Who did this?"
"Yes, my mother."
"She was pretty handy then."

In her armchair, arthritis crippling her hands,
wool inching through her fingers,
over, around, back, repeat, purl, plain,
row by row a soft chainmail appearing
into something we'd live in;
that other women would say,
"That's lovely, Lorna."

Hours, *hours*. "I'll just finish this row … "
Would be midnight, the house solidly asleep
and she under a cone of light,
the occasional click of needles.
Her skill, Royal Easter Show level.
She quietly proud. Her art—and what it required
—attention, time, the self-forgetting—
all the calculus of love.

Somehow, inattention maybe,
the jumper falls from the nurse's hands,
the one she'd troubled over.
"This pattern's tricky.
Like the one I'm making it for."
She said, without looking up.

At the Interment of My Mother's Ashes, Bundanoon

There was the funeral, its faces,
associations, recollections,
a kind of warmth.
A congregation stumbling
bullied. The organ hammering grief.
Noiselessly, the hearse slipped into traffic.
Tea, talk. Those drifting off, with promises.
The too-busy clean-up.

Today, we walk in through the low gate,
bracing against the first shock of wind
from the Gullies. Her grandchildren keep close.
As if warmth might deflect the confusion
of loss. Its fist.

Find the wall—names of friends, fellow churchgoers.
In some, the engraving already fading.
And see hers: the plate shining,
like a new face in the choir.

I trace my fingers over her name.
A name, among other names, in a wall,
now to withstand the abrading weather,
and despite promises, our faithlessness.
My children, raw in the wind, hug me.
This is the funeral.
We together, we apart. We close, we alone,
stand by our cars until awkwardness
makes us break.

III. "ENTANGLED"

About Clothes

The Weave

Getting undressed, ready for bed,
I become entangled inside my clothes

and note how I panic. Limbs
snared in the wrapping black.

My breath, a bird fluttering in a bone cage, fearful
as when, as a child having surgery, a mask smothered.

Only cloth, I know—the world breathes
the other side of the weave,

a thread's breadth away. Still,
everything is just a breath away.

Undressing

For the coldest days, checking stock,
   I'm bloated like an astronaut,
larvae in a freezer suit.
   It's fantastic! Cosy as!
One could easily be naked
   and not believe how
beyond this skin
   the knifing cold undresses.

Difficult though is undressing—
   confusion trying to edge the wadded bulk
off a shoulder's ridge. Or,
   bewildered where the body, this me, is—
dumb like roots in the thick of earth,
   Like thought clutched in the clay of words.

Undressed

Once, caving, I was aware
  how immoveable the earth.
Disinterested, unbreathing.
The world was rock.
  My breath the limit of me.
  Clothed, I was naked.
  I was stopped. Stripped.

Good and Faithful

How compliant! Under my hand
they bend and crease,
compress and kowtow.

Then, just as easily they spill
and like drunken sleepers lie
awkward in a mangle of their limbs.

Still, they're steeped in us,
we in them, old friends.
In each, a stain, or a joy

They give body to what they cover
—or what a body wishes to reveal,
then, uncomplainingly, retire

when as lovers, each in hunger,
needs the body to uncover before
we discover what we feel.

Guileless in their cut and drape,
unwittingly, they betray our age, our pocket,
the class we are or want to be,

or, in wearing the florals
of a foreign perfume,
where we might've been.

More on Clothes

At Arm's Length

From across a paddock
I'd know it was him.
Wearing this blue coat
a slow craft working,
bending, bent as the wind lay into him.

From its cuffs his fingers appeared
thick like frankfurts, as he grappled
with the foreign skills of a farm:
the intransigence of wire,
the struggle of a ewe.

Today, my fingers search
for a foreleg bent back.
I pull the lamb,
out into a snowy day.
At arm's length, his hands.

Indelible Ink

In hospital that last time
on his clothes in block letters
& black ink—"ERWIN"
like the serial number
of someone conscripted.

Malaria

"Memories linger in the blood, like malaria ... "
(Geraldine Doogue, ABC RN, 13/1/2018)

There were those little yellow pills he kept
amongst the Derris Dust and Rogor
in the garage, which we were frightened into
not going anywhere near.

Why hidden? Why there?
We just knew they were for 'Malaria'
about something far-off—New Guinea,
The war. That it shook him up.

And that was it.
He never allowed himself
to lapse into speaking, of anything
—spoils, women, slaughter, waste.

We, beyond his life,
are doing his remembering
that word "malaria"
infecting our blood.

"Banners Fill George Street ... "

Banners fill George Street in a chill April wind,
with names now possession of families
who keep them at the heart of their story.
Those with wry humour: "The Rats",
their brothers, "The Mice of Moresby".

Then those for whom a crowd is silent,
ones with steel, bamboo under the skin—
Sandakan, Changi, the 6th, Crete.
Some now are old words, beyond any memory,
engraved as print: The Boxer Rebellion, The Boer War,
4th Aust'n Inf Bttn.

Those names, their awkward syllables—Finisterre,
Madang, Aiatape, Bardia, Cyrenaica,
Bataan, Morotai, Leyte, Kalueng Riv., Tsimba Ridge, Finschafen.
My generation's—Long Tan, Nui Dhat.
A woman beside me murmurs a rosary:
Adele River, Marawaka, Gazelle Peninsula.
Hansa Bay, Tapen, Bush River, Matruh, Labuan.

There's the curious—Biscuit Bombers? Scrap Iron Flotilla?
The bizarre—A Carrier Pigeon Unit?
Some in code: NGVR, Angau, Dukws, RAE,
RAA, AWSA, NADZAB, Z Special.
In fact, it's all code: for what they couldn't speak,
and we cannot know.

As best they can these last pass
down George Street, and lowering,
are lost among tiring children
and our untested faces.

Remembrance Day, 11/11/22 Grabben Gullen

for Scott & Terri Montgomery

There were thirteen there.
I counted. All, bar one, older
than me. A few utes went past.
The Last Post ached,
fuzzy from the small PA.
A dog next door barked.
Silence, plucked from the day,
flowered for its minute.
Words were said, read.
The wind blew some away.

As I left, that space was space again,
empty as a stadium, weekday.
A lanyard slapped the flagpole lazily.
A wreath propped against the cairn had fallen.
Its plastic green a glossy, undying green.

The engraved names ask nothing,
Their letters like reefs exposed
Weathering the wear of our forgetting.

IV. " … A BRIEF HALO"

On His Farm, Not Long Before He Died

That afternoon, at his suggestion, we walked
out onto the hills above the house. Overhead,
a snow-heavy sky, torn and smoking,
as if a massive bombardment had ceased.
Everywhere, a birdless silence.

No sun all day. Under low, slushy cloud
last light was a clawing of fires. Scratched
against the sky the leafless sticks of poplars
lining the drive. He pointed, "Planted them.
Not long before they went."

Later, his whisky level in the glass.
Their faces, eager in nicotine-foxed frames,
the smell of a house too big.
"I stayed. Had to. They're on Crete, Greece …
Heard it's like here. All bloody rock.
Stinks of goats. Like pizzly wethers.
And rosemary.

Still, the trees have done well.
Your uncles 'd be pleased.
Don't you think?" Replaced
the stopper in the decanter, the decanter
in the sideboard, the sideboard shut.
"Enough. Good servant, bad master."

Chiming, the hall-clock searched
for company. A shock of cold air
as the dark accepted him.
And me, hearing him shuffle
as through leaves, down the hall
to the Box Brownie of his room.

FROM A PHOTOGRAPH, A LOVE POEM, BELLINGEN

for Jenny Deuchar

Against the eastern wall of a shed,
of a morning in autumn—nine-ish
—because dew drips from the eaves.
An early frost starched the ground,
the capeweed laced like doilies.

Three children shyly eager from the city,
and a poddy calf, like a gift.
Its unfamiliar warmth sleek
against bare legs. Each shiver
and little stamp of it an awakening.

This first moment beyond breakfast
entrée to the high gust, wind-silly delight
of holidays ahead, that unfenced,
will not exhaust until dusk, so that
later, when their lives harden,

they'll hold a moment
from these days like a pebble
taken shining from the creek.
And not say anything but know.
They giggle and squirm.

And their uncle. He almost smiling,
his hand, you note, ready there—
"Steady, young miss. Steady."
The kids lodge against him
as if this were forever.

That said, these were not my people.
I never met them, was never there.
They were hers and she is gone.
And so have they. They have all gone:
the kids hugging this man are in the city
they never were to leave.

And he of the good things: hands
resting on a kitchen table as if cupped
beneath a bird, stunned and trembling.
The voice, of water working in lost creeks,
out from the black of the tool shed,
"I daresay you could very well be right there",

who knew scale, and the limits
by which living things are bound
into the one drop of water,
and so knew cruelty only
as something curious, baffling.

He keeps to this photograph
the way his life kept to those hills.
And that look, which retreats
just as you feel the warmth of it,
like sunlight in the corner of a winter valley,
accepting me as if I were a friend.

A Quiet Woman

"Seriously? She's leaving him?
After, what, thirty years?"
            "Forty-five"
                            "Good Lord! They'd have been young.
Yes, I know … We're in the catching pen now!
Out there all those years, wasn't she?
Gave up too much? Her world, the coast, the piano?
Could've had a place in the SSO.
She has her children, grandchildren. Yes.
And I know, it's never black and white …
But those years she gave, they were hers.
For what? A kite on a string?
Even when he was there, he was absent.
And when he was absent …

Didn't recognise her.
A photo at a family reunion:
her kids back briefly,
bringing their children to be held
by an anxious stranger,
taken in a winter light at the beach
where her generation had flirted
in the accommodating sandhills.

I saw what a passer-by would
—a woman, now old.
Beauty replaced. Even so,
in the simple fall of her dress
she, her self."

“My Dear Man”

i.m. Brian Ridley

Dressed, finally, he comes from his room
bright as if setting out on a hike, “What’s
on the agenda today, my dear man?”

His pyjamas clownish from beneath the oilcoat
I’ve loaned him.
                    “Fencing. Where we were yesterday.”
“Of course. Very good. Very good.
What would you like me to do?”

“Would you step the distance from here
to that tree by the dam?”
                    “Of course. Delighted.”

And the wind catches his coat as he sails out,
while with pliers I attend to the strung wire
that seems as sure as a lifeline.

“497 paces if I’m not mistaken,” he smiling,
triumphant as a fisherman
with what he’s caught.

His death lost among the waters of days.
I stand in that paddock, grass at my knees waving.
Where am I now?

That man, dear man, lost and smiling,
striding away.

IN LONDON

for Lyn's friend Ken, a transcription of a conversation

He is where?
          In London.
He is inside that word—London.
From there he is telling stories
to keep alive what he knows.
          He is near to tears.
His parents are there.
It is their stories he tells:
those ample skies over a Kentish farm,
the bonehouses of war-ravaged lives
he couldn't save.
          This, a fiction,
which none outside that city
can comprehend. But he is filled
with a grief he wears as guilt
—for what he could do and hadn't.
          And now can't
—as what that city means
dribbles away from him.
          Except this—
a break in London's cloud
—a joke he makes, drily, against himself.
A brief halo, almost salvation
          among London's tears.

THIS CRAFT

for Chris, from photographs you sent

Already beyond the words which shape it
it's there, lying among tools and the mess
of its making but already,
the sleek long slow glide of it. Unpainted
it gleams in the satin of its wood.

Already, its freight is joy. It sings of the moment
when, after trial and bloody frustration,
you'd nutted it out. Each part gave up
its resistance and snapped, snug into being:
this new, honeyed thing.

And the language of its making—words,
as much as the tools you handled—cleat,
transom, coaming, sheave, mizzen,
—fragrant as shavings peeled from the shaping plane.

This ketch? Yawl? These photos
of where it's meant to be,
fully dressed and swan-gliding:
the human-scale of it.

And you, in the belly of your love. Ahh! Capt'n!
This craft is your poem, dear Chris.
Man of hyperbole and decency,
rolling in trakky daks, full heart, and subtle care.

Now though, you are out on a water,
in a craft not of your making,
where words make no sense.
And will not bring you back.

A Celebration

for Ruth and the Bell family

They are leaving. As am I. They embrace,
leave words for the wind to keep.
Friends, I guess, from a time after my time.
One passes near, enough to require recognition.
We were there for the same reason. Smiles
that sweet way, slightly more than perfunctory.
Disappears among cars.
                                        I hear sounds
of a party slowing, a fire dropping into its ashes.
The birthday girl, settled among her guests.
The grandchildren are tired of chasings,
they've had enough. Speeches, cake, done.
Voices murmuring like a motor idling.
It may continue for a while yet.

The photo montage cycles through:
her life, their lives. His face, his frame,
that grizzled beard appears. because
he cannot. He is elsewhere.
We know where. He does not.

Travelling Companion

Those faces you saw, maybe once,
which recur, alive, as in dreams.
Chance words, a sense
of a life, grained in their skin.

This man on a train to Sydney
—a station hand—clean white shirt,
weathered, tired, going for treatment
of a cancer.
                    "Years of spraying …
Buggered me. They couldn't care."

His voice, cracked as his hands.
His eyes looking past my youth, withdrew,
the way a screen around a bed
is a quiet separation. And acceptance.

That morning with its fog and the singing rails.
His face, lost in the crowd at Central.
The white shirt seen, then missed.
He somewhere, beyond that hour or so together,

beyond the blue haze of days,
the knock and shudder of cattle in the yards,
in a cab to St Vincent's. I see him,
as faces, lives, flicker in at the glass.

This man, his pale gaze,
those words among its silences,
sown in the grain of me, present
as reflections in a window.

A Breath on Glass

Something like the wind
has been at you, raking its claws.
Your make-up, your hair, though,
a defiant stand.

You are wandering
as through a house left empty.
In which room do I find you?

Although it is spring, it is cold.
There's the abundance of new blossom,
excessive and all-froth. But it is cold.

You are ragged in a barren valley.
Djinns whipping about you.
Standing at the window I realise

my voice is distant … I cannot give,
or make, or find—a door, or key, to a new day,
ticket or passport away from wherever you are.

Outside, against the bergamot-scented wattle,
a burst of blue wrens. Like flung grain they fall
to feed beneath this window.

All chirrup and bicker, flit and busy,
little as confetti. The garden chitters,
schoolyard-noisy with squabbles.

You smile, almost: a cloud sliding,
a brief light. A breath on glass.
It’s as much as I’ve seen all morning.

Swept by some urgency they’re gone.
And now, silence.
As when last notes cease.

There was a Woman

I have no idea of her
other than what my mother told me after visits.
I cannot check, for she too is dead.

My mother knew only what she gleaned,
and I'm not sure if seeking more I distort,
staining for the sake of colour.

From a well-to-do grazing family,
who could afford it, who didn't want
… the encumbrance,

was placed there, from puberty.
A "long-term resident", a fixture, as much
as any window opening onto the trim gardens.

She, who aged without being a woman.
Had to be a story. The staff, to make sense,
would garden and dress.

"Never trouble",
"Has her ways", "Happy enough",
"Tell she's from family".

Maybe the office, a Matron, knew.
Her name in the files like a tag
on luggage stowed in a back room.

My mother now dead ten years,
I am left with this story,
for a life held there. Words,

which blow away being spoken.
Like now. These—without weather or days:
    There was a woman, there.

Two Saved

i.m. Joyce Hetherington

The only evidence of a Mediterranean trip—
two apricot-dusky snaps from albums my aunt kept
the day we threw out her stuff. Sentiment gives way
to space. Anyway,

what did they mean? No-one knew.
Souvenirs of? The only clues—
KASMHIPIA (?) on a street awning,
IGOUMENITSA on the back of the other.

Two scenes: four men at a van, one
in uniform, the others bend, watching,
maybe suggesting. Absorbed,
they engage us too.

The other: the prow from the bridge of a ferry.
Feel the lift of the bow in the swell,
a mix of salt and diesel. And heat.
Its jaws grip your neck.

Waves slap the hull, supplant others
then fold under. That diesel-heavy moment,
those absorbed men—held, suspended
on the surface of film.

Though finished, the men linger, smoking.
The driver tosses thanks like a flicked cigarette,
submerges into traffic. Shadows from an awning
inch across the street. An afternoon dozes.

The bow slices toward a landfall
solidifying ahead. Passengers stir,
gather children, food. A woman in black
with chickens in a box sits unsmiling.

Caught at random, two images, chemical-yellow,
as the rest blow across the face of the Mitchell tip.
My eyes gave them life again.
I word into being what I cannot know.

Afterwards, Rain in the Car Park

A teacher of literature, now in the corridor, rocking,
"Take me back. Take me back. Take me … "
to everyone passing, to anyone.
Five months ago, he'd told me
modern poets weren't his cup of tea.
"Whan that Aprille with his shoures soote
The droghte of March hath perced to the roote … "
and punched me lightly on the arm.
"That's how you write poetry."

At the automatic door, like an athlete limbering
another man props, one foot to the other.
The door opens, closes, and he's still dancing.
Almost propels himself, then refrains.
Too hard. Twice more he stalls. Then,
lunges like a beast lurching from a bail.

The one who scurries, the one whose left shoulder rides
higher than the right; the transparent ones already illuminant;
he, of whom all said, " … such a sweet man";
the bristle-chinned women and the floral ones
with crepe-paper skin; the sexlessness.

Each on a raft:
faces turn, lift eyes mildly curious,
like ewes in a pen, then return,
shifting what's on their plate.

God! At what point do things turn?
I do not want to end in a charnel house,
with its gravy and urine-saturated air,
the cud-motion of mouths, the voice
crying in a desert at 4 am, the mid-afternoon quiet,
the descent, the genteel, awful descent.

I pass from my friend, the teacher of Chaucer and Milton,
who is dead, who looks at me as if he were my son,
and pleads, "Take me back". Forgets.
Asks an orderly the same thing.

The automatic doors seal behind.
Driving out, I release the clutch too quickly.
Surprised, the tyres savage the tarmac.
Rain spits hard rice.

The radio is playing Haydn.
I want fuck'n rock 'n' roll. Loud 'n' hard.
Hard.   No.
I want to hear nothing at all.
I want anything but this.

THE FISH POND

Visiting my great-grandmother,
The Little Sisters of the Poor, Randwick, 1960's

There was our weatherboard church, outer west,
Protestant; its Sunday light, lemon-clear about the pews,
but overwhelmed among lawnmowers triumphant.
And there was that massif of liver-dark brick:
Mount St Joseph. Catholic. Roman Catholic.

Everything, calm, assured: dark-honeyed light
deep in those brown lino floors; halls,
like shafts leading off to unknowable places.
Ceilings so high that in all that captured air
Heaven would surely be there, terrifying, terrible.
Everything faith-polished. A museum stillness.
Sometimes, rarely, like delight, sunlight fugitive
between blinds, slunk over the flesh
of marble columns, lustrous and serpentine.

To enter needed girding. This was duty.
Once inside, it seemed the days of the week
had been politely but firmly immured.
An ambulance siren, brakes jamming
beyond its high walls taught how silence
was built into the architecture here.
A reminder of the outside world—
its easy ignorance, the acceptance of sin.

To we, children of that plain church and the thin organ wheezing,
this was foreign. This was God's serious world.
Unsettling most—not the anonymity of the ever-gliding nuns,
the apartheid of their habit; shorn of adornment, faces rarefied.
No, worse: the statues of those forever tormented.
St Sebastian, his arrow-piercèd flesh,
at his feet, dogs adoringly licking his pork-white wounds.

Worst though: braving all weathers,
a forgotten Christ, baring his garish blue,
and red, and pumping, bleeding heart.
Veins like tentacles, plump with his sacrifice,
while his mother, pathetic in pastel-blue, looked
across the trim garden, fixedly helpless.

Too much: avoiding the residents,
their tissue-paper skins, their gaze clinging
like webs, we escaped
to a green pond in the stiff gardens.
Pale koi carp listlessly in motion.
Their bloodless eyes, watchful.
A flick, a glide, endlessly circling their days.

V. " ... THE MANY LITTLE BRIARS"

Hugh at Enmore

In the backyard of my brother's house
this little boy, my son, stands
lost in his three-year old life.
His face, of one
learning absence.
He hasn't words
enough yet, so
being inexpressible
his face is blank.
I cannot imagine
his lostness.

He does not accuse me.
Yet I stand accused,
at what I had done,
and have not been.

That photo, clear as witness,
utter as judgement,
for which any word
like forgiveness is glib.
Guilt walking beside me
like a warder, erect, unbending,
father to a feckless son.

at the Breakdown

Their bonnet up, gaping like a struck bird.
It is early dark on this back road.
But the man says they're right, OK,
as his boy peers from behind to see
who or what my voice might mean,
and hugs his father hard.
Seeing this, I hug my father too,
whose smell I still smell, as lifted,
I'd conquered all from his shoulder.

And I, a father, given love,
love what I miss, as we all must do.
My son, who at my shoulder
held me hard, harder,
who was here, has grown, has gone.

On Hearing of the Re-emergence of Epilepsy in Our Family

for Grace

There is nothing before its incarnation.
It's an insurrection the body doesn't see coming—
That terror—the mind being lost.
I had known this all my boyhood:

the pathway, like lightning, which chose
to cleave through all other matter
and strike the life that was my mother's.

It was in the sudden calm,
as when you look up on an ordinary day
to find the wind has dropped, the air still,
as if contained in a jar.

Then spookily,
a paleness, like the halo of a saint.
Not a light—maybe that background field
a power station has, humming.

Then for a boy the descent, as if abducted
and made be the one to witness
how this woman, his mother,
could dissolve into something other.

She'd crumple like dropped clothes,
jabber bubbling—words in looped repetition,
hopeless mantras, scaring me,
because I knew how far away she was.

Her head, wobbling puppet silly.
The body, which bore me, threshing like a caught shark.
The loss of dignity a woman would cringe over
if she knew.

And then, somehow, the adult world would find us.
A bed for her. The blessings of linen.
Our Polish neighbour and her love.
The softness of the dark.

The rest of the day for me, back at school,
not sure where the real world was,
like someone returning to a strangely peaceful land,
not able to speak of anything I had seen.

FOR ALEXANDRA

When You Do

You are cleaning up. Or out.
Whatever, it has to be done.
No matter how the ending
It's a new day now for you.

There's a photo of you on my cabinet.
You, of course, are younger.
Bright, potent with what your lives
Hopefully will become.
Isabelle hugs her dad. Sophie, a bub.
(Annie awaits her conception.)

So, what will you do with this photo
Of yourselves, bright and fresh,
Which you gave to keep me company—
Faces in a frame, the presence of love?

Checked, Picking Blackberries

Your children are elsewhere,
each day a drifting, worlds
you don't recognise.

They say, "love", even as you've done.
But they don't need your hunger,
the many little briars of it.

Which you know is what your love is.
They don't know about that, yet.
The sometime sweet fruit stains

your hands, beads of blood too.

Anticipating the Birth of a Grandchild

for Isabelle Claire

Ultrasound

It's human to work shape from the ferment,
fix the random, house the formless:
to see a face in the confetti of a crowd
the beaming Man in the Moon,
a Christ emerging out of the melting snows
or now, as I look, at the swirling cloud
of an ultrasound that's like a cyclone
tightening around its core, this image,
of you forming.
              Though I cannot make out your face.
              "That's a thumb, that's a foot", they tell me
but I can't make head nor tail of it.
              Your head is in the clouds,
You are somewhere else, are coming,
              coming to be.

This Face, Yours.

We're like those expecting
a relative from a continent
the other side of the earth,
whose tongue we cannot speak.
We're waiting for first sight
of a face, which once seen,
we know has always been among us.

Nocturne: Our Christmas, Jan. 2023

Their dust is already thinning.
The lights on the Christmas tree
are sharper now daylight's weakening.
Musk-like, soft grains of the dusk thicken
this room as the house settles and accepts.
Outside, the agapanthus is hanging on,
its blue withering, torn by the manic edge
of a summer storm scouring the garden.
Beyond, out in the paddock,
a black wall of pines resists
any such violation, while above them, far-off,
overblown gods perform, with stylised menace,
their pre-match ritual, bowing, posturing,
before collapsing as rain elsewhere,
miles to the north, out at sea.
Tired grasses, chaff-dry, but comfort too
—earth smells in through the window.
They will be getting near the turn-off now,
home a bit to go yet, the youngest already asleep.

for Annie Rose, Celebrating Her First Birthday, 4/1/23

It is a fortnight before your first birthday.
You were escorted into this life, five weeks prem,
Though no-one looking at you now would guess—
Sturdy as a member of the Politburo!
But a year ago we waited:
Your mother out on difficult seas of her body
And we here on land, useless as rags.

Today, I look out my window
At what I take for granted, and don't:
Trees I've planted, assured with blossom,
New growth of bright copper lances,
The melaleuca fizzing, shivering as wattlebirds ransack
Deep down alleys, emerging with pollen dusting their cheeks.

All this: contained in the body of a day!
I can't help but exult. There is being, and it is now. For your birth I sing.

VI. " ... ONE MASSIVE PAW UPON THE HEART"

The River

Smoke, and the voices of children ragged through trees
finds creases in me.
Here, in this unfamiliar place, absence
is something I hold onto.

I walk from the thrown nets of their chatter
to re-enter what I remember. All over,
clouds, fat-bellied as the Buddha, jostle,
indulgent as a bachelor uncle.

This is a world of hills in their yoga,
recumbent and languid as a lion's paw outstretched,
assured as language never is. Closer,
an arrested tumbling of bunched crowns

—olivine, and glossy as coal, rain-slicked,
the sinew of white trunks sloping to a groin
of water, musk and moist places,
where among the tangle of melaleuca and tea-tree

swarm blossom, insect-massed and humming white,
nervous with birdlife and flung about by fists of wind.
The nakedness of "is-ness"!
You'd be at ease here—

This world, your body. Your being,
like the ripe fruit of laughter,
like water spilling, lights flashing from it.
You said, "Being is enough

not to want anything more."
Easy said. Hear though, the river flowing,
its words lit and rippling.

Naming Each Room

Rounding a corner
it seemed to jut there, somehow nautical
in that dozing inland town. You hopped out,
went to the windows and quizzed the house,
while I hung back, disbelieving
I could be with you, torn
that I had children learning to be
without their father; their mother,
shredded by his betrayal.

Inside: the 10' high art-deco ceilings,
a kitchen big enough to dance in, and we did,
immediately, there, then, in our giddy,
careless, adulterous joy
among the clutter of another family—
the generations shifting—
But we didn't think too much. We didn't think.

An ugly, solid, proud house, a garage,
honest in its accumulated stuff
—a grazing family from the wool days,
bowls and golf clubs, an excess of gardening tools
for a tired yard, tired from bearing with
the false starts of old people, everywhere, pots
like the cupped hands of beggars, yet room
for chooks. ("I'd really love chooks again, Russ"
—as if somehow, they signified a new life.)

A bedroom so big our bed was a raft
shelved beneath heights of sandstone cliffs,
wallpaper flaking, mildew flowering.
The wide hall, as if always open to laughter
and flow. A sense too—the reserve of distance.
Cool as avenues of oaks. A sense of acres.
The bathroom: reminiscent of Central Railway
—fragile black and white tiles, black dado,
ugly raw tubing—fashion of the 1930's.

Big enough for two, it had its charm
—its light, late afternoon, the summer heat,
water in pearls down and over your breasts
and the jasmine along the fence outside
perfuming the steaming air.

Each morning I'd drive east, you west …

Driving past months later, still clinging,
I saw the new tenants sitting where we'd sit
each afternoon with a beer, accepting
brief release in the new air of a breeze,
and wondered what lives lived there now,
what it was like inside. If they knew of
summer afternoons after making love,
the pure shower, the scent of jasmine?
Were they happy?
                                I was. Sort of.
Not really.
                                And guilt.
What did they know of that?

‘The Day we Got Drunk on Cake’

after William Trevor

The ache almost gone.
That, of course, the saddest.

You would do anything
to have it back again.

So: the indulgence—
What is she doing now?

Does she think of me?
What could we say

if we met somewhere?
You suspect she has forgotten.

Though you know
you’ve forgotten most things too.

Except, of course, the primal ones:
her scent, a living thing,

as too that tiger padding in her name,
one massive paw upon the heart.

And the things you replay on an endless reel
of what she’d said you should’ve known.

Those words like the remnants of a party,
the alcohol beginning to wear off,

the cake in ruins.

Watermark

Stand, let it cool your feet,
allow it to shock your country thighs.
Stand and withstand. Wear the rush and thump,
the froth's nibbling chill, so that tonight,
climbing west beyond
the broken jawline of the escarpment
into the clouds' strung and dreaming coast,
the body still feels the Pacific watermark the skin—
the way you felt her hand's caress.

Wear the sea's flounce about you,
like a sarong; feel it, like lips
whispering on your flesh.
Let the skin remember this—
the way you felt her mouth, her hands, her body,
then even her heart withdrawing.
And tonight, inland, allow the buffet,
again, and again, and hear the words
the seagulls tore up over your head.

The Memorial Hall

A box of a hall made for echoes.
A piano sticky in its varnish,
stowed in a corner.
Around it chairs set like old women,
their feet wishing to dance memories.
Dust hazes down long columns,
submarine and slow.

In its silence everything speaks, not sings,
of the emptiness of an empty hall.
Like love when the loving stops.

Night Driving

I'm driving inside a globe of light
blown out before me. Beyond, all over,
the careless spattering of a cosmos.

High beam: a filigree of leaves, frost-silver, etched
as on crystal glassware, crisp against
the ill-set limbs of snow gums, awkward and leaning;

a suddenly melting snowflake of an owl;
propped stumps, ears pricked, erect as an alerted wallaby,
but mostly this, the dry sea of a road at night,

with its bow-wave and wake of dust and wind,
opening, closing, forgetting.
Cosy, this gravel-humming room.

Sometimes there's a glow on a ridge.
You steel for its assault. It turns off,
becomes a sheet of watery milk. A cigarette glow

then, extinguished. Somewhere ahead,
like waking, I'll turn at a gate,
my headlights shaping what my days have paid.

Now though I'm nowhere, wordless
and humming, consciously slumbering,
happy among the stars and the night-wind,

as if I were hearing your voice.

FOR YOUR DAUGHTER AND HER GRANDDAUGHTER

On the fridge the photograph is doing its work.
You are alive, young, and most dangerous of all,
assuredly beautiful. Your life is ahead
as you and a friend capture a photographer's attention.

Nor do you reach out to the future
—you, simply alive with days, potent
like bubbles waiting in the champagne.
We either side of a border,

equally blessed in ignorance
of what the turning light holds.
Although I, who did not know you,
know, after the shutter clicked, holding

you ambered in this cameo,
how your days took the shape of a story
now told which you lived
but could not know.

You flare a smile at the photographer,
your heels clipping firmly down Pitt Street,
as your daughter attends to her granddaughter
in a day that's made up of moments,

any one like a photograph.

Setting the Scene

On the screen a simple world,
a hard country. The setting, murder-grey.
Music such as there is, whistles
the wind's tune. Every face
wears the wind's mark, scored
like Millet's *Man bending over a Hoe.*
Close-up, their flaws, obvious as any
we've learned to read and misread.

As the credits slip, we disentangle
from the couch, fumble to bed,
going from what we know—
(the murderer unmasked,
the mystery revealed.)
And, in the refuge of the dark,
turn to each other, and to what
we don't or can't or daren't.

I Hear

Outside, a stiff breeze shifts
the bells of the wind-chimes
she had given me.

Each clink a clear voice,
distinct as hers,
clips of sound

now, and now, and now.
And between, around,
shaping each sound

— silence.

And now that her days
are elsewhere,
this is what I hear.

Their Secrets

for Lyn

"Our parents are entitled to their secrets," you said.
So obvious, yet I hadn't thought it. My parents? Secrets?
Were there more than what I knew? Of course.
Those unreachable days, before ours: their days.
Of personal myth, private griefs, heart-buried joy.

There's our keenest hunger in wanting: any light,
scent, shade, colour. Of things hinted, unsaid,
or simply not understood; poring over
such photos as there were, imagining. Hunting,
say, the back of a lowboy, some letters, hoping

they light the blankness of before—faces unnamed, the where?
Of places; of loves, lovers, their glow, their disappearance.
Even after, cleaning out, a discovery, "What's this?"
Any thing. Always, smoke thinning in a midday air.

Their days—at best, tenuous in the mesh
of what's thought is remembered, or embroidered.
Whatever was we won't know, we barely
knowing this me, shivering in its web.

And despite your clear sense, you too search
among what might remain,
held in words long silent,
that they explain a torn space in you

a lifetime has sought repair.

VII. " ... WHAT THE WEATHER BRINGS"

Day Off, Off Botany

From there can you see me?
I see you on the beach.
I hear your kids squeal as little waves splash.
And those girls, bikinis, sunglasses, beautiful, eh?
Today, Sunday, sunny day. My day off.
But we cannot leave. Ah! Those yachts
between us. So free.
Your city, nice. From here it sparkles.

Our days are here. Diesel is our air.
Our heart beats under our feet.
Days tumble like laundry, in the water behind.
We watch TV, watch each other, laugh white teeth,
speak a little Greek, use English, dream Tagalog.
Do not dream. Always smile.

I am on this island, in your bay. Home?
My heart. Where my children are. I am here.
They know me from remittances.
They outgrow the photos above my bunk.
Last time, Cecilia said she wanted to be
an airline hostess, but I hear will be
in service in Dubai, later this year.
Geraldez, good boy, likes basketball.
Muscle now under his t-shirt.
O! Mother of God! Keep him
from the easy laugh of hard boys.

Our days, like clothes. Water is water.
Most time you do not feel the sea too much.
The ship, big enough. Is always working,
like thoughts I wake to,
turning over where my kids are.

at the Archibald Prize 2016: the Young Archies

He is the father. He is slender. Vietnamese.
I sense self-effacement.
Allowing me to look,
he steps aside.

His daughter has drawn his son.
She too is reed-slight.
Diffident, teenage-shy
—not in a sour-pouting way
but confident somehow. Maybe
knows she's done something pretty good.

The father is proud. He points, "This, my son.
She, my daughter."
"She … ," he gestures a drawing hand,
"The artist. I am famous two times."

He smiling, that his life
should have been allowed this much.
Later, I see them waiting in a queue.
This man, slight as a reed
which gives with the wind.
They, leaning into each other.

IN PASSING

i.m. John Betts

Stepping out the front door I step
where late summer, Frank 'd been found.
As when showing me over his farm
a dear man asked about my son, Hugh.
"I too had a son, Hugh. We just passed over
where he was killed."

Or visiting, say, Culloden, Villers-Bretonneux,
beneath your feet, every step, bodies have been.
In the mizzle-damp soil sticks to your shoes.
Different but same—the flattened grass
where you'd sat is where lovers chose.

I think of when, after passing between
the automatic doors of a city hospital,
(How they shut so shut!),
I'd exchanged clothes for a gown,
and sat on a bed, now mine,

looking out over the stacked city,
the traffic passing down there.
Saw a couple kiss, then part at the lights
where I had crossed.

3am. Waking to the Radio

At this hour as minutes in their chains drown,
                                something globed drifts upward.
                        Wayward, diffuse, it disappears.
Then—in dribs and gaggles,
                        like a flock loose-strung across a far hill,
swung in long cables through oceans, others,
                                tendril-soft as climbing beans, feeling
to latch.
        One catches.
                Then more, clutching.
Some harden to pattern, script flowing across tiles in a mosque.
Consonant and vowel twining like snakes in their helix of mating:
        one distinct as the ring of a horseshoe on stone,
                        the other bending, bowing, sinuous as dance.

Amorphous they form, aggregate like spawn. Morph into pheme,
become babel—Aramaic? Amharic? Catalan? Xhosa?
Or just an infant's milk-clotted gurgle?
A race-caller's pigeon-scattering scramble? Possibly.
There're clues you catch.
                        That tattoo of air-shapes
—from non- into sense. The 3am news forms
like a ragged platoon.

A new day, the self resuming,
as if the body were dressing.
The world in its skin again.
Remember coming out of anaesthetic,
that moment, "How're you feeling?'
Like Apollo, out from dark nothing,
reconnecting with Houston, a voice, words:
the world is now, and very near.

Coming Home, I Hear the Radio

In 2013, the year of your birth, Isabelle

It is autumn, 2013, good soft rain,
and now, a peach-soft air.
Scent has returned,
the nap and fuzz of new growth
beneath a thatch of dried summer grasses.

And there's the radio I hear
coming in from the paddock
—clotted sound separating,
becoming words, words
announcing the world.

And though you don't know this yet,
they'll frame how you'll be known,
a self you'll sort of recognise,
as you wheel through the seasons.

Listen though, to how your being
hums a wordless, gentler song
as you wear what the weather brings.

FROM WORDS HEARD ON THE LAW REPORT

"We are entering deep water. Everything is unclear ... "
(ABC RN, 25/10/2011)

There is this, now:
spring rain hesitant
on the tin roof,
or the astounding iris
which, even in the rain,
cannot help but speak its blue.
Or the sense of her,
come into the room, here,
behind my chair.

Other than this—the skin,
each day we enter deep water.
Everything unclear.
At best, this slight craft
—sounds our breath shapes
in passage between us.

Like those now, words
over the radio—alive,
freighted, lost. But heard,
signals across deep water.

FROM A DREAM: MAYBE A TIMBER CAMP

Look up from the table
	at which you are seated,
at the figure there.
	Before you, dark in the door,
his feet in sodden boots,
	snow melting in a pool
on a wooden floor.

He stands—unspeaking—
	maybe awaiting orders
or brings news on a piece
	of paper, limp in his hands.
Who knows?
	He is a voice now, outside,
one among others, at ease,
	in the way water rejoins water.

It's the day beyond you'll remember:
	a cold, blue light
illuminating from below.
	All about, silence.
A country deep in freshly fallen snow.
	The squeak underfoot.
That shock—
	the antiseptic air,
and drifting,
	a scent of pine,
to which you wake.

Hume Highway Song—Northbound, from Gundagai

On the highway after rain. Before me—hard red hills, morning-soft.
This world shining!
Passing a behemoth, fabulous from another world—
like those freighting Apollo spacecraft. I squeeze past.
It, at a drugged sloth-creep, off to do serious work, somewhere,
to alter the face of the planet.
                                        I zoom. Sun-fuelled.
See a magpie alighting onto a dead branch.
I like that word, "alighting"—the lift, then easily settling.
I imagine its lyric into the autumn air, burbling, a ripe nectar.
Liquid and living …
                                        Pay attention!
The tarmac demands it—cracks, subsidence, edges, the archaeology of litter.
Now, the tyre-song hum, a lathe machining into a day, peeling freshness.
Above: birds in aerial dogfights
(do they face cracks negotiating their highway of sky?)
pass grey nomads, with their snail's shell wobbling,
rocking as B-doubles slam with their wake;
pass billboards,—close-up, see how a smile
is the rictus of clown heads swivelling at the Easter Show.

Right now, no radio. The only words, my own—tumbling with the light.
Then shyly—small voices—hand-written, propped, cradling names.
Singing grief, what else can love do?

Pass a stock truck—a beast's head, wide-eyed, between the siding.
But I am at a standstill!—Tradies zip past, zoned into their dream, radio pumpin'.
Pass lorries—I like that word too—it's from the days of my grandfather,
who saw them come into his world, as he handled his team of half-draughts and dray.
His world had scale.
But these ... towering like an aircraft carrier, dockside, labour toward the maw of the gods they feed.

Hang on!
As if entering a tunnel, within its shadow, an industrial roaring.
They keep pace. Feel the pitch, scream and thrum! The trance of wheels!
Then out! Ah!
Heading now up into the country of the low cloud, the black-green hills,
the bitten rug of tired pasture flecked with grey-white sheep, two weeks shorn.
Sense now, the air, dampish. An easterly freshening.
Light, already with winter's edge, buffs the windscreen.
Almost there, the day, older, seems settled.
Back there though, it was autumn, fresh, unspoilt. A new day then.
And there was that bird. *Alighting*

Skydiver above Camden

Heading north on the Hume Hwy, spy there,
beneath a membrane, pale as a new moon,
a comma hung,
swaying.
Peg-shaped, a pendulum, suspended,
it disappears in and out
of the light.
Afloat in the thrilling updraught of fear,
everything he is
is thin as fabric.
Being this free, he is out of his depth.

He learns contours—a cloud's wisp,
the earth's sleeping muscle,
and, as air whips his body,
the island
he is.

Diving is release.
Nothing can be built or demanded.
Only,
a terrifying joy.
Its shock and buffet and sway.
And a stillness.
Helpless,
he loves it.
Delighting in the shock,
this willing plunge in the pure air
of death-terror,
this hanging man
is as vulnerable as when he awaited
his birth.
Helpless.

Still, this speck has it over us,
sees what he is entering;
of cause and effect in its traffic;
weight and fact and consequence.
Beneath his dangling feet,
earth—
still minutes away—
where absorbed among us
he'll wear our awe and fearful gaze,
calm, uplifted.

Balancing

A mare's tail sky, a road of talcum dust
withering to a white horizon. Nearer:
trees shaken of their leaves, stricken like old men.

And above the stalks of a season's grasses
a hard light. It picks out
the blue in the little Virgin's chipped statue.

As if the centrepiece of a table set so,
a rosette of sun-bleached buildings glare,
sharp as salt.

The black of their shadows is solid
and cold. Light doesn't stand a chance.
The head of a beast noses from behind

a wind-eaten corner, a trophy on a shield.
It pauses. A foreleg extends, tests.
The off-hind leg, lifts, hesitates, then is placed.

... Takes weight. Blades of grass
are snatched, as if stolen. You notice its eyes,
liquid as begging children.

Eyes which mirror those men lounging
beneath an awning's deep shade,
who gaze to the horizon, then flick back.

Voices, sudden as summer lightning.
One of them turns a blade in his hands,
presses the point into the meat of his palm.

Tests his flesh. They look out
into a silence which sucks sacrifice
from every living thing: work, desire,

prayers, breath, returning nothing.
Under a sky this indifferent,
a balance, as at the point of a knife.

VIII. "AMONG HANDS ... "

New on the Skyline

The Convent of Our Lady of Mercy

Into a flannel-heavy afternoon it declares itself
—in spikes of disruption and consequence.
At first, a scent, has tang, is acrid, and we wake.

Even at a distance, feel the writhe of it.
Among cloaks and billows flame
alive in the pleasure of its work.

We watch waves ripple, filmy and distorting,
or how, when thwarted, improvises, cat's-paw teasing,
then resumes, spewing new visions of release.

At once, everything swamps under sound.
A sundering, rafters breach then surrender
to haze and memory. A vaporizing of histories,

rooms of air liberated back to air.
Once held in the attitude of prayer,
fingers claw an unfamiliar sky.

Scale

Old St Paul's, Wellington, New Zealand
for John and Jane Foulcher

Midday. We enter, into the usual cold of a church,
the usual scent of emptiness, that sense
one has arrived too early or too late,
or shouldn't be there.

Even so, an effulgence—a port-wine warmth
embered in wood. Thumbprints of light
like votive candles, a dull gleam off surfaces.
Overhead, not painted heavens

but a bare frame, as of a boat upturned,
ribbed and straked. Fitted for work.
And of a scale—that of hands, skill, craft.
Attention, and hours. Modest, a quiet voice,

speaking of shelter, of trees in their forest.
In the stillness, resilience. Light,
a spangling as on a leaf-thick floor.
And sense too, voices, in the fact of work,

distinct as bird calls in the silence;
the singing of their tools.
We, unsure being here, assured though,
being among hands, and the work of hands.

"All Felled, Felled … "

On the Destruction of a Sycamore Tree, Hadrian's Wall,
and TransGrid's Plans for my Farm

Obviously, an affront or a challenge to them
That solitary it grew and withstood three hundred years,
Spring-leafed, winter spare, a quiet reminder
Of the slightness of their mortality. And so, cleanly
Their saw sated their irritation with the years of its sure growing.
I say this from a continent uneasy with the gifts
We have taken and laid waste to, while singing
Our fake bonhomie, "She'll be right, mate."
I say this looking out my window to where, soon,
The work of this lifetime will at some hour hear
The arrival of men and then, a chainsaw tearing methodically
Into the life growing there. And afterwards,
The crushed silence. The scent of eucalypts
Persisting for days, and useless.

this Time, a Village, in the Ukraine

From here, over the slate-tiled roofs
a cloud disperses, becoming fumes, hair-wisped,
as beneath, an orange-bright flare is a dress
gusted upwards, flowering white
in the instant of its purity.

We can't know, can't feel, the shock, the heat,
but do know that, at that point, there,
what will be known, tears bodies from their lives,
children gaping open, children no longer children.
Somewhere there.

And this was now, then.
And now, images on my phone collapse the tenses.
Though we distant, are not burnt. We allow ourselves shock.
We, useless and safe, as those flowers fade.

IX. "THIS REPUBLIC ... IS ENOUGH"

Here, this Farm

Pure arc, this dome
a polished stone.
This silence, everywhere.
Our music, our sea
for each day's ark.
Our scoured home.

About Farm Welding, Mostly

Snap your visor! Anonymous as an astronaut,
mythic as Ned Kelly, you're brutal as Darth Vader.
Under the mask it's mine-black. Sleep's O loveliest colour.
The breath, your only companion. Become your eyes,
you're pricked for any pinprick of light.

You've rehearsed this on backs of envelopes, in dust on a shed floor,
Still, it's a surprise: a hand, your hand, that's distant from where you are, strikes.
And—not one sun but all suns, all light that ever could be, is!
Pure. Absolute as darkness ever was.
No tenor in the sweep of his aria so overwhelms like this. Nothing.

It fascinates as when descending at night over the coals of a city,
say Delhi or Manila. Under your hand solar flares leap, licking the dark,
lava, with its coffee swirls and fumes, gouges canyons as it flows.
I swear I've seen a cool Buddha sitting in his cave of yellow lotus there.

Heat! The purity of. I feel the slow tumble of coals—giant cobs crumbling
from Port Kembla's coke ovens that terrified as no sermon could,
ever since the walls of their huge breath assaulted my face, cleansing it.
Safe behind glass, as down on the steel-mill floor thunders molten rivers,

I learn of how the lonely would step a step.
Faceless, they resurface in dreams for a lifetime, voiceless
As Shadrach in the Fiery Furnace and every other martyr after.
The calm of sati widows too. They cow me with their self-possession.
I am being baptised. I sense

what had overawed me in Arthur Mee's Encyclopaedia
—Tubal Cain towering among flames! Now, uncertain
of what I hold—through my hand energy thrums,
—spit, spark, fuse, hum down there in molten light.

It's like what tremors through you, when on a dam wall,
beneath your feet floodwaters plunge catchments of cold damage.
Farther, at the flash's margin, spatter is like gibbers strewn
about the Moon. Already, at the rod's burin-point,
a fading down the heat-gradient to human red.

Lift your visor. Ahh! Breathe! Air, fresh as spring pasture!
Resurface. Step out of the workshop dark, knock the scale off.
Turning this new work over, a seam grins,
refracting rainbows, gleams like a cut jewel
or a bead of dew trembling on a leaf.

There, in the Rain

It is there. As suddenly as that.
Through the open door, out in the paddock,
the bulk of it has become that space. A Rothko

of saturated black, a map of Europe stained deep
over its backline, beads trickling in piddles,
the bull solidly, noiselessly, is there.

Wearing the rain, he stands and does not move.
Huge like night terrors I met in childhood:
a presence black in the black of sleep,

which overwhelmed with nothing's menace.
The bulk of him. He moves.
The dark remains.

THIS RAIN-SOFTENED SATURDAY MORNING

Each day, I pass the huts the Irish family built
—a rammed earth kitchen, a room for Maria and Pat—
the boys by the fire.
                                        Neglected. I've no use for these
adzed timbers aching to fall.
                                        And they're gone: a family, a name
elsewhere among others. Once in chat, yarns too,
around, even beyond the district—unheard, unspoken.
The seasons shift everything: new counties
take shape, names dissolve.

And those people who have no graves,
my feet step where theirs parted grasses and passed.
Every now and again, their tools, egg-smooth,
chipped up by the harrows, or this elliptic,
dense, grooved stone pick, scarred
by a disc scraping over it, almost buried again.

And now: a morning of rain, in faint pencils,
a gauze across the greening lawn.
Like so many other mornings—lovely … but …
I read the death notices of those I've known
since I came.
The hush of soft rain. Softly. Soft.
And it stops.

Of an Oak Tree in the Paddock, Early Winter

On fire, this oak tree radiating gold leaf,
is the El Alamein fountain lit.
Gorgeous as a Klimt mosaic, showering carelessly,
wind-washed, this undressing
in spatterings and littered spoil.

Days later, a haze almost smoke,
cobwebbed in grey.
Beneath is to be under fan-vaulting.
An architecture of nerve, kinked and shifting,
framing jigsaws of space,
like the promise of different views
a house offers, raw in its dream;
so open a pigeon might easily fly through.

The day comes, pays court
with decorations of hours and birds.
The weather tries on moods,
by turns wilful, coquettish, sullen.

Accepting the indifference of cattle,
each standing in a quiet sadness,
it casts, like lace, a net of fine shadow.
Dressed as it is, this republic,
clean as sculpture, winter-spare, is enough.

Examining a Yabby

Much more than a spring day's powder-blue
this lacquered, gem-brilliant blue, a yabby
in its segments on which a cormorant fed.
                    Two-toned actually—
the inner-side—old ivory with small pits pricked evenly
and a blush of salmon-edging near the lesser pincer.
                    The pincers!
Imagine them at an industrial scale!
Almost over-engineered, museum-monstrous,
plates like medieval armour. And along each ridge
tiny serrations, that finishing touch of subtle design.
Each refine to a hooked tip. Almost kiss.
Side-on there's the cruelty of a smile.
All fashioned for this: Precise. Sudden.

Dragonfly

Lain as if a gift left, a bejewelled, glittering thing.
This enamelled, hornet-yellow brooch, as brilliant
an ornament as a Pharaoh might allow,
varnish-stiff, preserved in the amber of death,
singular as all deaths are, on the seat of my ute.
                                        In flight like a Dornier, that nubbed
gridiron helmet of a head, that length of fuselage trailing.
Now, delicate in my hand, hardened out of air,
shining in words almost too heavy,
—evanescent, diaphanous—their closest cousin—gossamer
in its fields of spider threads,
                                                            —all sheen, glint, ephemera,
those veined, improbable, cellophane wings—
now shimmering, now vanishing,
in and out of the light, flirting at a razored edge.

Beginning with a Rosella

In a pure arc, $y=x^2$, it curves
to fold among leaves. Poised
it stands in air, in a flare

of red and blue.
Still as a photograph.
Settling, a branch flexes under it.

This on a clear day, ocean-blue,
shade-stained green edging down to the foreshores
of a sunburnt paddock. And so still.

The slightest shift lifts a twig of new growth
then surely returns it to stillness,
like glassware reset upon a shelf.

Schoolboy larrikins, a pair of magpies swerve,
flee through a gap of light. Their cries
linger, aching.

And now, this stillness, how dense.
You would not know that time is passing,
that daylight hardens.

AND ON A DAY SOON

There are the shit days, purely that,
those days of sleet with its knives
as you kneel with a ewe,
all the mechanics of birth
when grief's wrapped in it,
elbows caught; a tongue blubbered thick
from a head flopping against the arse of its mother:
the dismemberment, the smell, her low moan,
the anger that you were too late,
            or the bitch had got down
            where you couldn't get her.

So that there's relief as on a day not far off, one hopes,
when Spring delivers itself of its scent, that lift of air,
and light is strangely new again. And clean-cut,
the muscled hills, distinct from the sky.
And warmth and grass brilliant
and you too are new-filled.
                        Hear birdsong everywhere.
                    Stand and look and breathe this.
                            You've earned it.
                Like income it will have to last a year.

The Difference

Today, riding past it is normal quiet,
everyday farm quiet.
A tyre flattens the edge of the stain,
clogged in the dirt.

When I saw her, it wasn't good.
Yes, she was old, she'd lost a calf
but her uterus, God,
a pulpy blood-black jube,

carbuncular, looked as if chewed.
The gun's telescopic sights,
bloody useless at close range.
Took a guess.

A shiver, the mountain-side slump
and collapse of her,
surprise in a moan,
the shocked cough.

A gaping hole.
                    Silence.
Not quiet.
                    Silence.

Two Poems

A sense of it

Alert. Always.
The slightest difference—
Scent, shade, shift of presence.
Fluid-limbed quick,
All nerved to this, their world,
Which parts and closes,
Alive with chance.
A shadow shivers in the grass.
And drifting, that sharp stink.

Lapse

I come back, and blown like litter, a nest
Of ash-grey down, as if spilled from a pillow.
A head, the eye, clouded as marble.

Cattle in the paddock mooch near the fence.
A wattle bird scrapes its unpleasant voice.
A light breeze reorganises leaves in the garden.

Inside, on the kitchen bench
Eggs I'd collected yesterday.

Surgical

The windows are open to catch a chance of air.
A blowfly homes in on the bed lamp
answering whatever light compels.
Its zithering, its fan of air twitches my nose, my cheek,
as it crosses, recrosses. Its blundering maddens.
I swipe, slam a book
where I thought it was.
Turn off the light.

Outside, leaves in the apricot shift.
Then, in the far corner
where the ceiling is another world,
its voice—different, higher revved.
And does not alter.
The web shakes, tears, but doesn't break.
Above my head, a delicate attention,
voiceless, and surgical.

So quickly ..., So ...

i.

This happens quickly,
too quickly. And in slow motion.
Today, they're perched, managing balance on the quad bike.
Feet, I notice, dancing, keeping sure-footed on the tray,
as they're travelling at a fair clip, negotiating that bend
as we meet them.
Unbalanced, reacting to the sudden braking, one jumps off.
And we are there.

And she is a thud beneath our wheels. Already,
her eyes retreat from this day.
Her body, heavy as a rug, with legs awkward,
sticks beneath a collapsed tent.

ii.

You see it as you did then,
a lifetime ago—outside Sydney Uni. Was it drizzling?
Certainly grey. A couple, in their now-found cocoon
of each other, take a punt.
                                        A lull in the traffic, unusually still.
                                                They dash. He stops,
pulls back. On his left, alive in their invulnerability, she
continues.
A car in the third lane can do nothing. She becomes
acrobatic.
I still see her head bounce as if playful upon a bed.
The window of the bus frames it. Behind glass
there're no voices, and we slide into traffic.
I grasp at what I can. Her joy …,
Her eyes realising …

"Because, like the Weather ... "

Because, like the weather, it colours this place
you don't always notice. Maybe it's
the careful way something's said and not said,
friendly enough, often with a smile;
no matter how long you've lived among the same hills,
know some of the gossip, the better-known yarns,
you can't be trusted to understand.
    How could you?
    Today, this:
They'd been seeing it for some time,
even caught sight of it padding by the back door,
its stink down at the chook pens,
but now it's here, in a cage they'd set
with one of the lambs it killed.

There is panic in the froth of saliva.
Eyes engorged with brilliance.
    Their dogs. The fox.
They bay and snap at either side of the bars.

It is sweat-matted, concentrates its stare
on its newest threat, swivels, and snarls,
and tears at air. Is lost in the mash of its fate.
    One by one
a new dog is introduced
until terror extinguishes with a yelp.
The cage, silent as the hills,
    as all witness is.
"Best way to blood pups," he says.
Trusting me with that much.

Weight

The daily constant is weight.
It's the cost you pay.
Over time the body learns
how the balance tilts.
Think grapple, heft, negotiate, accept,
—with humour, with bad grace.
"Alright stay there! Miserable bastard!
'll get yer, tomorrer".
Like prising this year's crop of basalt rocks
before they rip the sump out of the ute.
Or jacking up that ute without a jack, over
the rocks, newly there, which you didn't see.
Or taking on fallen limbs contorting
in their physics, twisting your arm
like a canny wrestler.
Or, as when a pulled calf, like a huge clot
among its birth-blood, knocks you,
A over T, in the blubber of its rush.

Win some: the weightless "Ahh!"
when what you've lifted is new,
even sculptural, day's end.
Lose a few. That sinking "Ohh!"
when you find her standing
over what she's lost.

Hill Farm

Wind-crippled, checking his ewes,
returning to a house with its photos,
bloodless and distant in their frames.
His children elsewhere,
their voices different
on the phone. "What's that?"
Didn't catch you."
Cards with drawings come
on birthdays. School photos
like a test. Each face he searches
to find what he can.
Saying they want the best,
"Dad. Sell. Get a life."

The ewes have begun to lamb.
Tomorrow, he'll lay out some baits
now a fox has taken a couple.
A bit late, he knows.
Get a bit of wood in.

Today though, a break in the sleet,
a light burned the tips of the snow gum,
like that voice from the burning bush.

Getting Warmer

Bent, I feed the flame.
          Shyly, like a wary animal,
it licks the paper's face,
          is almost velvety—
a gown of Imperial purple
with a fluid hem of kerosene blue.

Testing, like one's foot at a cliff's edge … testing …
          Stutters, regathers,
inches on its belly like a fox.
          Then, the way a crowd
releases itself—
          Whump!
          Petals unfold
          lazy-quick like papadam.
Gorgeous and neon-garish.
          Everywhere, flaring …
The Mardi Gras swirl of it!
          Like marauders looting,
the thrill, spit, and bite,
          tearing through cell walls.

Shutting the fire door,
          my face raw as sunburn,
words lick, little flames flicker,
          grinning,
"Not long now, you know.
          Not long."

X. " ... ARE MOVED INTO LOVE"

“Good to See You Above Ground”

i.m. Ron Price

Not often in town, I realise those I’ve known
have changed their faces, wear the ones
by which their grandchildren will remember them.
Shy, many emerge now only for their own funerals.
Those they know are those they’ve known,
and that is enough.

Marbled in them, hockey and ‘roo drives,
flagon muscat, feet frozen in the potato ground,
wood raffles, early Mass, third Mass, and snow,
the ring of cousins marrying close and closer.
“Nine kids, but the foxes got a few.”
One child too many given away.
Nothing said. But remembered.

“A big heart and a big wood pile,
that’s what you need”. “Nothing fancy—
we’re spuds and buttermilk people”,
Ireland in snow-burnt purpled noses;
canny, hard judgement of strangers,
harder of each other; and common enough,
the deaths of boys in cars.
The following of a hearse.

Talking of which, if there were more than
a half-dozen cars parked in Goulburn St
a weekday you'd ask, "Whose send-off?"
Now, every day seems like Saturday except
it's the weekenders who wear riding boots
while asking where's the best coffee,
keeping iPhones handy should they be stranded,
their Pastoral Co. logo fresh on the Range Rover,
the mud too.

And those I've known as names
strung behind other names, those
who wear days of high cloud unaffectedly,
recognise me, as if meeting after a long absence,
someone from Back Home, the Old Country.

FOR ISOBEL HEATON

Driving back I pass the Gurrundah graveyard,
with its newly-red mound settling
on the winter-brown grass
and think of you.
                                        Bright, clear-eyed woman,
who readily gave us reason to enjoy
that we are alive, with each other,
—though some might be "a bit tricky",
 or "surprising", as is our capricious weather.
                                        All amusing though.

Your grave borders the paddocks
with which you filled your married life.
You would have seen those sheep grazing.
I hear your laughter,
                                        and wave.

This Is It. a Reading from Paul's Letter to the Corinthians

i.m. Michael Hewitt. For Natalie Hewitt

Late, they enter. With a touch at her back,
the man guides his wife to one of the few empty places.
She brushes lint from his shoulder.
They settle among us.
                                        We wait. This is it.
The light is honeyed; there is a peewit
outside, calling, wincing off. Hay-making season.
The smell of grasses drying.

This is it, big man. Your people are here.
This is old Crookwell. You'd have done this yourself,
big-hearted man, any number of times—
St Mary's, your church, where you were married,
from where you'll leave.
"She'll be big," we say, "Get there early."

This is it: in the quiet river of the responses,
in the answering silence, in each body murmuring
with the words which hum our mortality.
This is it. Taken out from the day
we again know something.
Despite our coarseness and forgetfulness,
touch death, and moved, are moved into love,
even in the casualness of a gesture.

Never more so than when that slight, shy woman
stepped to the lectern and gave clear, assured shape
to those words of Paul as I had never heard before,
for you, her brother-in-law, you big man.
Those words read, spoke.
And being spoken, breathed life,
love.

Two Deaths at the Abbey

i.m. Kathleen Hughes

While I sleep, she is dying.
She will not receive visitors.
As she has always done,
this she is doing alone.
By co-incidence in the same place
as had my father.

I remember the long watch of that night
and the moment. 4.17 am.
The numbers of the clock face,
black standing out from the white.
And it was finished.

I remember silence, shrunken to this room,
complete as an ocean. Elsewhere,
the shifting of bodies in other rooms,
murmurs, mutterings, cries cut off.
Outside, there was the stillness
of the frost and the first stirrings of a bird
announcing its survival,

while we watched his slow, unyielding labour.
And only we there, to sense
a weakening of the dark,
grey sifting behind the blinds.
It was finished.
It was as if we were returning
from a mine into the strangeness of a day.

She too is elsewhere:
morphine feeds a measured peace.
There is no other world now than this:
the body jettisoned of anything it was.
Each moment distils the one before.

On this raft, she and her God,
whom she holds, close as the breath.
They, twinned like dancers—
even as pain works its sure knife.
The slow, quick-quick, slow.

Tonight, I pray that she …
No … that *you*, Kathleen,
you who wished to spare us,
will be held, truly,
within a fold of wings,
because there are no arms …

as you slip, alone,
in that place where others,
each in a failing body,
wait out their night,
while we, who do not keep watch,
turn and ignorantly sleep.

Sainte-Chapelle, 2019

Early evening. Blue weakens to a dishwater grey.
Stone walls adjust their tone accordingly. We queue,
Shuffle, enter. Slightly disappointed. Is this it?

We climb the winding stair. My knees question
The effort. Ascending, a hint of colour tints
The right-hand side of the wall.

A sense of a pale light increasing above us.
And of people ahead in the hum and murmur.
What is there? We climb.

And, as if mounting a crest,
Before us, all around, brilliant and flooding,
Something beyond anything we have known.

And "Aahh!" in-spired, the only response.
One in a community of the favoured,
Each of us stands rapt, isolated, happily contained.

We are immersed. And are not ourselves,
Being most surely selved.
No one speaks. Over everyone, light.

A Passenger

i.m. Lorna Erwin nee Trist

Cosseted, cosy, glazed, in a bubble of a car,
being injected into, through, this revelation
of calm order: fields, uniform, laid like tiles.
Everywhere, the unfathomed depth of green.
Mondrian blocks of yellow canola, the tarry
and piss-reek from piles of manured bedding
outside barns, and tractors, huge as ogres,
bearing down, filling the rear-view window.

I am being driven through England. It is May. Spring.
Not drought-shrunken autumn I left three days ago.
Capsuled, I'm submerged in sunken lanes
beneath dense small-leaved foliage, where through chinks,
light in a strobe-flicker dazes, like dazzle off chipped water.

From what had been names, now, there!
"So, this is Balliol!", "That said 'Adlestrop'!"
Or fleetingly, a horse, stamped high on the chalk,
huge as myth. Ageless and atavistic.
Is there relief from so much history? Everywhere,
Vaughan Williams, Samuel Palmer, Jerusalem.
Blood tilled into tidiness, a loam of self-assurance.

This my first trip, maybe my only. I doze.
The undemanding light soothes like a calm voice.
Absent from daily life, I'm a passenger,
lit with the gifts this soft country gives,
not speaking, just receiving.

Lulled, I think what it must have been like
for my mother, felled by a stroke.
Unable to do anything. To not speak.
Only burble from a tracheotomy.
Those brown eyes gazing.
For a year to the day. Each day.

THE GRAVELLED YARD

from a line in Patrick Kavanagh's "The Hospital"

Two words in a line, and they pitch you,
to a corner of a grandmother's house
which you knew. Yes, you *did* know.

There, a frangipani numb in the winter sun,
its stubbed fingers, grey, tumescent,
bent awkward, among where the ashes were flung.

Over the palings, the forbidden outer yard,
where before you were born, his team waited,
steaming in the morning air.

Shuffling, chinking, the chaff-fullness
of their breath, "Steady, steady there",
Pipe-smoke drifting.

And she, when you knew her,
in that dead house
—rooms deep as caves, desiccated and Arctic.
Life, a kerosene heater fluttering stink.

Long dead, as are her children,
she comes, arthritic, not smiling. Just worn.
Frangipani and harness give up their scent

Of flowers and sweat.
In the dark, wheels crunch
the *gravelled* yard.

We Visit Her Country, Co. Down

All day, must be getting closer, threading lanes,
criss-crossing, somewhere here surely.
We, alert for any clue, cling to hints—
in names we'd heard my father's people use,
of a land elsewhere—Ballynahinch, Dromore, Saintfield.

I scramble to accommodate what I'm seeing
with how I'd imagined a place, which for generations
bred those who've shared my name.
Only the deep green everywhere settles.

The afternoon wears. The sky, pale as a thin sheet.
I sense this day will resolve to impressions:
of landscape, a district, the sprawl of countryside.
Then, that name—"Carricknaveagh Rd", pieced
from beneath a bramble of wild roses, speaks.

In its letters I hear their accent—serious, rolling, a music
which had been to me so very Irish, *Northern* Irish.
Shaping the sounds, I remember how it spoke of "us",
—a line singing out across water, catching light.

"Yes!", my sister says, "*That's* where I stayed!"
And speaks to a man on a mower. "Aye,
I'm cousin to them but they're not about."
His accent like rock firm on rock.

"So, we're cousins then," she who carries our history
like the Torah. "Go down there", he nods,
"that's all Scott land there, and the church,
your grandmother's house, on the left, going down."

And going down through the dense green,
shadows thickening, leaf on leaf, me on hair-trigger.
This is where they worked, wore the seasons,
drew water, slaughtered the pig, courted,
prayed their fierce, hard prayers, and hungered

for what America, Australia might give.
We meet another, closer cousin living where
Anna Scott had grown. Genial enough, remembers names
but resists in his pleasant, deflecting way.

We have come this far. Here, the birthplace she left.
It's now his—this man on whom we've intruded
with our hunger, from a past he coincidentally shares,
cares less. The green world withdraws. His day closing,

he smiles, rises, follows his wife indoors.
Uncertain, we stand at the gate
in the denying daylight,
with names in our heads like useless keys.

Boardmills Churchyard

Finding the church, we pass graves.
"I met them when I was over here last time."
Now, ran-tan, and sweaty, a youth group
is racketing its deconsecrated space.
No sense of what had been poured
into the thin, hard music of psalms lifted there,
the unutterable prayer murmured into hands.

A youngish woman asks our purpose.
We point to the graves, "We're looking
for the Scotts." She, surprised, in the velvet
of her brogue, "Well, I'm one of those!"
My sister and she ply names, deaths,
quick biographies and frayed lineage.

To one side, I look at this woman
we've met by chance. The face
of my grandmother, photographed in Lisburn
before leaving this place forever,
looks across three generations.
The linen-fair skin, the fine thick hair, the steady eyes.

A mizzling rain dews the car park.
We do not move. I realise I'm as close to,
and as far from, Anna Scott, who worshipped here,
was courted, left, and with her children,
is now dead, ten thousand miles away.

We break. Say what we know is goodbye.
What more could we have expected?
Those known, in their graves.
The living, met by chance.

She brushes a strand of hair
fallen across her face and waves.
My grandmother, as I would never know her,
standing there, receding.

Bellaghy

i.m. Seamus Heaney and Les Murray

Capricious as spring is, blue among tufts
of cloud. A fresh wind nips our faces,
a tarry smell drifts from chimneys.
We enter Bellaghy, looking for the church and his grave.

The finger board, it seems, set to deflect the casual,
points as much to the hills. The priest about to drive off,
"Sorry, my son. I'm only filling in," and winds his window up.
A trickle of voices around a corner offers hope:

another graveyard? At the furthest reach,
just before consecrated ground lapses,
tucked away, his grave. I kneel.
Damp grass stains my knees.

A man, like a bachelor farmer, approaches,
asks, and finding my purpose, "Ah Seamus!
A cousin you know. A good man. Good man. Yes.
But not one, you know, for the church."

I cannot believe I am here.
Beneath my feet, his body.
Poems grown from this earth
on my breath, his words living,

as the sounds of ordinary life
murmur just beyond the churchyard.
And this, just a few weeks after learning,
in the nowhere of mid-flight,
of the death of you, Les.

Me, foreign in the land of my forebears,
two generation removed, absent
from a country clamped in its second year
of another drought. And now, your death.

A mist drifts in, as the churchyard resumes
its compact with silence.
Damp is clammy on my collar.
I kneel on this, our common earth,

knowing there will be no more
other than what we've been given.
Those gifts—often stunning,
miraculous even—

like that promise of a rainbow,
ordinary, and absolute,
and unconditional,
lit with the assurance, *Noli timere.*

The presence of Creation. Always.

"*Noli timere*"—"be not afraid"—the last words by Seamus Heaney in a text message to his wife shortly before he died.

Full Circle (Glasnevin, Dublin 2019)

i.m. Mae Vanderschaar

Just beyond these walls the traffic slurs unceasing.
Here, among the neat paths, the dumb marble,
people walk down lanes, stop, then resume searching;
garden staff with tools and purpose; the sound of language
clipped and muted; the wind with an edge.

And I am unmoored, in another country,
here to touch what began on a page
and taken flight, broke me open, rupturing me
into the rapture and scent and full-blown blossoming
nearly fifty years ago.

At reception the young fellow is courteous
but wet and blank. By chance an older guide hears
and curtly says, “I know where. Follow me.”
Then points and leaves.

                                        A weathered obelisk,
names graven, crumbling, becoming faint,
I use my fingers to spell out: “Fr Geraldus Hopkins”.
Among the bones of others, his.

                                        Fifty years and I am here:
the traffic, the sour wind, the acres of the dead.
I don’t know what I wanted by coming,
and so, stand, feeling stupid, and begin to recite
to the pikes, the weed-tufted ground, the disinterested air,

“I caught this morning morning’s minion … ”
Wishing they were tears. That he might hear.
And know.
            He, dear, delicate, difficult, o’er mastering me font
of whatever in me is poetry.
            For that I came.

THE OTHERS THERE (GLASNEVIN, 2019)

Few of you would've been as starred as he
Few possibly as scarred, though I can't tell.
No-one can. Now that you're all there
In the same grave, your names weathering,
Stone crumbling at my touch.

I came because of him, who was my love,
If love is what sets your life alight.
Words, our tongue, he set singing
As iron ringing on an anvil: a bird flew,
Water flowed, giving itself over and over,
Beauty in-dwelling in everything.

And you, who had no words like his,
Who lived your hours in the same service,
Your bones mixed with his,
What can be sung or said of your days,
Their weather—of joy or drudgery,
The heart broken again, and again,
Vigilance against sin, the hope of resurrection,
Or how you too accepted a silent bed
Which your Christ kept for you?

Back Here, a New Place

Where I've been had no country.
Today, aware a day has shape,
I feel I've stepped out,
feeling the brace of a cold air.
This place, where I've lived
most my life, is new.
Certainly, a change of season
but somehow the breathing paddocks
are foreign, tilted, reoriented.

The shape of everything requires attention.
And every time is the first time.
Tell me names so I may re-enter
what you know, and learn again
what I must have known. And
eat the bread of acceptance.

An infant, I am unsteady, distracted.
I step out, in the same, different air.
I touch things. And marvel.

SIGHTINGS

Currawongs, Moss Vale

Despite the yellow eye,
hard and unforgiving,
it is the lingering syrup
of its call, early evening,
among pines, out of mist,
drifting up the escarpment,
like a curfew, saying,
"The dark is here.
It is now cold, and
this is no place for you."

Lyrebird, Macquarie Pass

Out of the mist,
like a tatty shuttle,
then scutting back into
the damp silence,
its scrawny tail trailing
thin as dried fern,
a lyrebird skitters across
as we ascend the Pass.
A scuffle somewhere
in the moistness
of leaf-mould and half-light
—voices of worlds
and words not its own.

"P-r-e-e-w"

When entering a paddock
spiked with rank phalaris,
my son, then small, carried a stick,
larger than himself,
scything it about, shouting,
warrior-fierce syllables
like a haka,
so's not to be frightened
when "P-r-e-e-w!"
quail burst,
small land mines
exploding at his feet.

Out from the Cumbungi

A thing fugitive,
always spearing away
from wherever I am,
a Japanese snipe, flecked
in the tones of a rice-paper screen.
It must be gone, must, must.
Its bill, a needle pointing,
urgent for home.

Bower Bird

Among pegs, plastic milk-tops
in his grass and bracken thatch
he attends not as a shopkeeper
arranging his wares
but as a petitioner,
desire beggaring him
while she inspects.

What does she want? He waits.
Traffic from the town rumbles up
to here on Mt Alexandra.
Lights go on in the street.
He waits, bobbing.

In the morning, I find the pegs
pearled with dew
like toys left out in the rain,
the work torn down.

Narooma

A sea eagle in a long low swoop
slices the glass of the lagoon,
splintering the surface, strikes
a fish and carries it with its mirror image
to a tree, and beyond this morning.

Little Eagle

That day, this autumn, ploughing for winter feed,
suddenly, a stain of shadow
circling over me, so near
I could see the tattoo of its markings.
Its clear eye.
                                        Unperturbed,
it swooped low and over
the tractor a few times. Satisfied,
two, three wing beats, it swam
leisurely to a stand of timber nearby.
                    I knew then that distance
which keeps all things in awe or fear.

The Eye

Once, inspecting the lambing paddock, strange,
like a weathered root somehow there. Then closer,
I could say haughty but just staking its claim.
With one feathered trouser, it heraldic, refuses
to be intimidated, a wedgetail on a lamb.
Its eye grips till I leave the paddock. Fair exchange.

There, at the Window

After a dry season, some rain
and Bogong moths flap at the screen:
their eyes iridescent as they cling,
urgent to feed on the light.
Then, before me, flaring—
like a cape spread out,
the window fills with wings.
An owl coming out of the dark,
bares its barred chest.
Falls away, comes again,
and then again.
Each time, its talons hooked
inches from my face.

Funereal Cockatoos

Rain coming! Pleased as prophets, they cry.
Funereal? Ha! In sorties, like Lancaster bombers
they pass over as if in complete command,
then knowing my hakeas, settle there, stripping branches.
You hear them cracking nuts, at ease,
like bikies who've taken over a pub,
as more, slow beat, slow beat, slide into a feast.

A Visitation

Within view of my window a grapevine
which hardly bears fruit. When it does,
has berries, small, bitter and big-seeded.
In the yellowing leaves one autumn,
after a season when all things had done well,
a ruffling unusual for little things such as wrens.
Noisy, greedy sounds, unconcerned
there could be any danger. There,
as gold as Yeats' gold enamelling,
a golden oriole emerged and perched
for a moment. Never seen before or since,
it, held there, among a mosaic of dying leaves
and the bitter-sweet, useless fruit of that vine.

Yellow-rumped Thornbills

Not a wind-blown scatter
but rather like a net flung,
this midge-cloud en-masse turns
as if a drawstring's pulled,
and collapsing, now decorates
the leptospermum
with dots of yellow,
loud with chirruping and chatter.
Like the flicker of lights coming on
in the windows of a city tower
its many voices, indistinguishable,
and one.

Of Plumage

Which?
Cadmium white sulphur-crested,
—donned completely like an acolyte,
an ascetic's purest sensuality?

Or, if they were not so raucously common
the delicacy of roseate pink,
against a doona-plump grey—
galahs wheeling against the sunset
then settling, murmuring,
would be all the balm
the spirit needs.

Then there're Gang-gangs,
in their Kings' School uniform,
alert, confident as merchant bankers,
red bonnet defiant of a Canberra winter.

Or glimpsed brilliance
—a sacred kingfisher flashes.
Too quick, all that colour, aflare,
a jolt like the kick of an electric fence—
so apt—a spear and sacred.

But most, this: the finest cross-hatching
of olive, blue-black-touched, and rufous too,
all velvet to a brooch—an eye ringed
clear as honesty, fine, pure in its name
—Silvereye.

The Grey Shrike-thrush

Of all I want to sing of you,
who nests each year
in a tea box in my garage,
whose song is spring to me,
whose plumage, soft grey
is such as choristers wear,
so as not to detract from
its liquid praise, filling life
after winter's drear.

Grey Fantail

I tower like the blue genie in *Aladdin*.
My stubby hands are claws
And you are death-still within them.

My thumb massages your breast,
It rubs the fretwork of needle-fine bone
So easily the skin could tear.

More present in flight around my room,
Which you mistook through an open door,
You fizz and scissor-whizz

Until between a window's clear treachery
And the cloud-menace of me
You collapse into grams of grey and fear.

Still. Not even trembling, you wait.
In the stillness there's something
You cannot disguise—

Faint against my thumb, a pulse.
Feel it, fierce in its necessity.

Before Light, a Magpie-lark

A sound. A couple of sounds.
A perforation of the dark
when there is no hour.
A voice searches, the way a child calls out.
Anxious, it weakens
as soon as it calls. Is absorbed
in the dark's smother.

Notes which are brittle, nervous, not enough
to unravel or flute into ribbons and arias.
Neither is there a flood of generosity.
A song but not singing. Not sweet either.
The ripeness of a grey shrike-thrush's lyric tops it,
effortlessly, ad nauseam; currawongs,
hard eyes in sleek tuxedos,
indulge their fugues of liquid melancholy.

Plaintive, lost. This thin voice
is the simple truth of this place.
It speaks of sticks, of noon, of distance.
"No-one here," the bird cries, "No one."
The wince of an axe working free,
it carries over the years, from a Villawood schoolyard,
1960s. Always far off. And further off.

Or a Saturday afternoon, a small voice
somewhere in the expanse of a carpark.
In the new subdivision it cries, searching
through the gums left standing. Then ceases:
that emptiness, that waste of hours.

This is Radio Australia,
relayed from the heart.
Seeking consolation.
At this hour this is far from certain.
I listen. It stops. It, lost to the dark.

Within Reach
by Russell Erwin

for Lyn Miller

Originally the two poems in 'Anticipating the Birth of a Grandchild' appeared in a little presentation book, *Notes Toward an Imminent Arrival*, published privately. I thank Margaret Swieringa for her support.

A number of these poems have been published previously, mostly in *Quadrant*. I am indebted to its literary editor, Les Murray, for his generosity and support. Several have been included in anthologies: *Best Australian Poems 2017*, ed., Sarah Holland-Batt, Black Inc. Carlton, 2017. *The Quadrant Book of Poetry, 2001-2010* ed., Les Murray, Quadrant Books Sydney 2012.

For their care and attention, I am especially grateful to John Foulcher, Keith Harrison, and Penelope Layland who generously helped shape the manuscript into something better than it was. I thank too Alan Gould and Geoff Page for their collegial acceptance and support over the years.

First published 2025

POETRY

ISBN: 978-1-7636009-4-2

BOOK, TYPSETTING, AND LOGO DESIGN
Mountains Brown Press

PUBLISHER
Life Before Man

Gazebo Books
PO Box 375
Summer Hill
New South Wales 2130
Australia

gazebobooks.com.au/life-before-man/

2 4 6 8 10 9 7 5 3 1

This book was made possible thanks to Anthony Mark Day

COVER IMAGE: *Cinnamon Tea-Cake*, 2023, oil, and glass on linen, 26 x 20.5 cm, © Phil Day

ISBN 978-1-7636009-4-2